1-25-10

RAW HEAVEN

AND LIVE APART (1980)

RAW
HEAVEN

POEMS BY MOLLY PEACOCK

VINTAGE BOOKS

A DIVISION OF RANDOM HOUSE, INC.

NEW YORK

FIRST VINTAGE BOOKS EDITION, SEPTEMBER 1984

I am grateful to the Ingram Merrill Foundation, Yaddo, The
Virginia Center for the Creative Arts and The MacDowell Colony
for their support. I also want to thank Phillis Levin for her advice.

*Portions of this work have previously appeared in
the following publications:*
The *Antioch Review, Calyx,* the *Georgia Review,* the *Little
Magazine, Mississippi Review, New Letters, Paris Review, Pequod,*
the *Poetry Review,* the *Princeton Spectrum* and *Shenandoah.*

Five poems have also appeared in book form in *From Mt. San
Angelo: Stories, Poems & Essays,* published by the Virginia Center
for Creative Arts.

Library of Congress Cataloging in Publication Data
Peacock, Molly, 1947–
    Raw heaven.
    I. Title.
[PS3566.E15R3   1984b]   811'.54   84-40162
ISBN 0-394-72707-X (pbk.)

FOR MARC-ANTONIO CONSOLI

CONTENTS

RAW HEAVEN

THE DISTANCE UP CLOSE

All my life I've had goals to go after, goals
in a molten distance. And just the way snows
in the distance, dense and white among groves
of bare trees, lessen as I approach and show,
not white, but a mix of mud and leaves among rows
of breathing trees, the fantasies that rose
from my young mind, guarded against my foes'
mocking by my own mocking, lessen. I know
what I've approached, and I am very frightened. It shows
in my slipping face in the melting present. Goals
far off are fire and ice, like a walk through snow
toward a blood-orange sunset. But there is no
perfection like that in coming up close, no
purity in intimacy. Embracing the world, nose
to brow with what we've got and lost, hugging old sorrows
as they fade into mud and leaves, is like shedding clothes,
is like lovers saying, *let's-take-off-our-clothes*.
The word is made flesh in their bodies: does is knows.
The world is made flesh by the snows
fading, then merging into mud and leaves, goals
of long ago emerging among trees in rows
in a distance molten as the world comes up close.

THE LULL

The possum lay on the tracks fully dead.
I'm the kind of person who stops to look.
It was big and white with flies on its head,
a thick healthy hairless tail, and strong, hooked
nails on its racoon-like feet. It was a full-
grown possum. It was sturdy and adult.
Only its head was smashed. In the lull
that it took to look, you took the time to insult
the corpse, the flies, the world, the fact that we were
traipsing in our dress shoes down the railroad tracks.
"That's disgusting." You said that. Dreams, brains, fur
and guts: what we are. That's my bargain, the Pax
Peacock, with the world. Look hard, life's soft. Life's cache
is flesh, flesh, and flesh.

JUST ABOUT ASLEEP TOGETHER

Just about asleep together, tenderness
of monkey-like swells of grooming ourselves
just about stilled, the duet nonetheless
whispers on, unshelving everything shelved
by the day. A head shifted by nude arms
into its right place soothes the crooked habits
of the body. In lips that talk out of harm's
way is a softness known only to rabbits
and sleepers. It shifts them from the almost to
the genuine: a heavy sleep, black and blank,
the void before a dream. At some cost to
this ankle, that hip, one head, one armpit, a shank
slowly curves, a back turns, an ass is fit
to a belly and two bodies lie frankly
foetal, knees drawn, crook into crook, wing by tit
in the orbit of sleeping. And blankly
shifting and waking without waking
is that much touch that is our sleep making.

OLD ROADSIDE RESORTS

Summer is a chartreuse hell in the mountains,
green after green after green, the wet smell
of possibility in everything. "Doubt him?"
a memory of a friend's voice asks. Yes! "Well,
why do you love a man who's in a tangle
you yourself would never be in?" So I am,
the hypotenuse of a triangle
watching the other two sides in a jam
of history and pain and veils, like veils
of green washing over the mountain spines
on which perch the broken-down summer jails,
pale boxes that housed Chasidim in the pines
years ago. They're richer now, and go elsewhere.
So mice, squirrels, spiders, and racoons stay there.

The mountains are like the backs of friendly
dinosaurs who, if they heaved in their sleep,
would throw a small car all the way gently
to Syracuse. Moist follicular trees weep
and chatter. I used to be married, goddamn.
Like him, I was in the tangle I'll never be in.
From the third side I had to see the sham,
the last side, the last window to see in.
Inside stolen time and through time's arches
are these places, webbed and dusty now,
mosquitoes humming among the old porches,
overgrown, sloping, askew. They are endowed,
the gnaw-footed dreams of animals' lairs,
with the vacant stateliness of claw-footed chairs.

THOSE PAPERWEIGHTS WITH
SNOW INSIDE

Dad pushed my mother down the cellar stairs.
Gram had me name each plant in her garden.
My father got drunk. Ma went to country fairs.
The pet chameleon we had was warden
of the living-room curtains where us kids
stood waiting for their headlights to turn in.
My mother took me to the library where ids
entered the Land of Faery or slipped in
the houses of the rich. A teacher told me
to brush my teeth. My sister ran away.
My father broke the kitchen table in half.
My mother went to work. Not to carry
all this in the body's frame is not to see
how the heart and arms were formed on its behalf.
I can't put the burden down. It's what formed
the house I became as the glass ball stormed.

WHERE IS HOME?

Our homes are on our backs and don't forget it.
But we don't stay in them; we think them.
Homes are from our minds. Once I tried to fit,
repairing through remembering, the stem
of a favorite glass back on its head. No loss.
A man in dirty overalls swung down
from his truck grabbing the bag of shards to toss
into the maw of his truck. To me he was a clown
reaching a powdered hand into the garbage bag
and plucking out the glass intact. Thus in my mind
I'd everything I had. And please tag
along home with me now. The paths are blind
with wet new grass behind the rusty gate
where my low blurry child home lies in state.

OUR ROOM

I tell the children in school sometimes
why I hate alcoholics: my father was one.
"Alcohol" and "disease" I use, and shun
the word "drunk" or even "drinking," since one time
the kids burst out laughing when I told them.
I felt as though they were laughing at me.
I waited for them, wounded, remem-
bering how I imagined they'd howl at me
when I was in grade 5. Acting drunk
is a guaranteed screamer, especially
for boys. I'm quiet when I sort the junk
of my childhood for them, quiet so we
will all be quiet, and they can ask what
questions they have to and tell about what
happened to them, too. The classroom becomes
oddly lonely when we talk about our homes.

LONELINESS

It shines as broth in a cup meant
to be brought by both hands up to tempt
a waiting mouth under a light shines, low,
somewhat harsh, then flickeringly half lit
as it, itself, is consumed. Slowly the toe
of the drinker curls in a gentle fit
of tension and satisfaction, as in
the reading of a novel's last pages.
Were the wet mouth to speak, it would be
in a voice that hasn't spoken for ages
because the little voice is so far inside
and the way back is a long, ill-lit ride.

SHE LAYS

She lays each beautifully mooned index finger
in the furrow on the right and on the left
sides of her clitoris and lets them linger
in their swollen cribs until the wish to see the shaft
exposed lets her move her fingers at the same time
to the right and left sides pinning back
the labia in a nest of hair, the pink sack
of folds exposed, the purplish ridge she'll climb,
when she lets one hand re-pin the labia
to free the other to wander with a withheld
purpose as if it were lost in the sands when the Via
To The City appeared suddenly, exposed:
when the whole exhausted mons is finally held
by both hands is when the Via gates are closed,

but they are open now, as open as her
thighs lying open among the arranged pillows.
Secrets have no place in the orchid boat of her
body and old pink brain beneath the willows.
This is self-love, assured, and this is lost time.
This is knowing, knowing, known
since growing, growing, grown;
revelation without astonishment,
understanding what is meant.
This is world-love. This is lost I'm.

VIOLET DUSKS

Everything used to be symbolic. Say,
turning the clocks back, there was a symbol.
Everything was going to get dark and stay
eternally unlit. Winter was simple:
it was awful when every day ended
at five o'clock. But I like short days now.
Short days are fine. Early nights, befriended
by a season's predictability, bow
like beautifully formed embryos within
the shells of short days which are, themselves,
each a surprise in a known time. (The din
days had made as they slid off their shelves
at five P.M. and smashed so horrified me
I felt the world had smashed. The autumn spree

had ended and what I hated, the stark
walls of my office and my house, had come
to entrap me with their government mark
of lawful acceptability. Numb, dumb,
and very, very dark. Turning a clock back
even an hour toward the violence
of childhood led me to hate time.) The lack
of a day hour now means a night hour: violet
blush in back of each black building and lights
of headlights and streetlights glowing with the day
going past the lovely gradations of sight's
exhaustion from lavender to gray.
Life's so short it makes the icons cower.
A grown woman loves any light or dark hour.

THE SHOULDERS OF WOMEN

The shoulders of women are shallow, narrow,
and thin compared to the shoulders of men,
surprisingly thin, like the young pharaohs
whose shoulders in stick figures are written
on stones, or bony as the short gold wings
of cranes on oriental screens. Lord, how
surprising to embrace the shortened stirrings
of many bones in their sockets above breasts! Now
what I expect, since I've long embraced men,
is the flesh of the shoulder and the cave
of the chest and I get neither—we're so small.
Unwittingly frail and unknowing and brave
like cranes and young kings, the shoulders of women
turn to surprise and surprise me again with all
their gestures of renewal and recall.

THE LAND OF VEILS

Beth carefully carves the pears into her
plastic bowl while I talk to her mother.
Beth looks directly at our eyes, but we blur
into the foreground, and Beth blurs toward another
land of her own. "You are very grown-up indeed,
slicing that fruit so nicely," I think she'd like
me to think before her mother and I speed
far away through the waters, then land and strike
our tents on the shore of the chest and thighs
of so-and-so's ballet instructor. The talk
of women, the thousand dim kitchens I sighed
in the backgrounds of, hoping just once to stalk
the animals of my mother's friends' desires—
Beth is doing it just right; she does not
commit the sin of commotion; she aspires
toward a grown-up task (fruit salad); she will blot
herself all up until she is a ghost
among the veils and veils and veils of women
laughing in their tents along the coast
of experience, the ripe persimmons
of acknowledged fantasy in their hands,
until the land of her own we believe Beth is in
is among our burnishing lands.

NORTH OF THE EYES

Sure it's hard to have sympathy with a
healthy pair of arms and legs and hair
growing bountifully and a belly, a
belly on the oversized side, and a pair
of listening blue eyes over a mouth,
a smallish mouth, that is telling you it
can't go on. "I can't go on," it says. South
of the lips, the chin is firm. The eyes are lit
but not about to cry. North of the eyes
a hand with infinite gentleness smoothes
the skin across the brow as it removes
the strands of hair that fell into the eyes
which looked so clearly out at the world as
the mouth talked. That gentle hand is part
of the same body. It is hard to impart
sorrow from such clarity, since a face such as
this, wiping its own brow without a hope
of having it soothed, says it has such hope.

TWO CUPS ON THE TABLE

I can only rearrange furniture
in our tiny fantasized apartment
in Florence, seen through a curious aperture:
the lens of hope, its constant restatement
of every old fact about us.
I remember this and that and try to fit
everything we own in far small rooms, fuss
muss, shit! I'm lonely, I can't help it!
Out here on my thousand-mile frontier I grow
more barbaric every day! Soon I'll be like
my neighbors. Save me! Can you hear me? No?
We'll lie intertwined till we look alike
through all the nights till we're a hundred and six!

The stamina of my hope: a window open till dusk.

SQUIRREL DISAPPEARS

From the fence to the fire escape to this
tiny unexpected yard, his manic
tail quick as the fin of a maple seed is,
flip, flip, a squirrel stops for the scenic
view of sky, wires, restaurant rear, and dog.
Then off again. The air's brief clarity,
like an empty open hand before the fog
of belief disperses the disparity
of "here" and "gone," takes a chip out of time,
like a chipped minute out of love when a word,
a hard word, twitches and is off, its crime
the dissolution of where we'd been lured,
the tiny unexpected yard, love. Empty,
then brief bottomless disbelief in plenty.

THINGS TO DO

Planning and worrying and waking up
in the morning with items on the list
clanking like quarters in the brain's tin cup,
this and that and what you might have missed
or who pissed you off, suspends you in a state
that wishes and hopes for its goal like some
little one wiggling in a chair who can't wait
for when her legs will reach the floor. The numb
knockings of anxiety are like the heels
of sturdy little shoes steadily beating
on upholstery. It's how anyone feels
having been put into a chair, meeting
responsibilities from a padded perch
too big for anyone's ass. As monarchs
we make ourselves small and govern in search
of what we'll grow into. Except we are
as big as we'll ever get and have gone as far.

SMELL

The smoky smell of menses—Ma always
left the bathroom door open—smote the hall
the way the elephant-house smell dazed
the crowd in the vestibule at the zoo, all
holding their noses yet pushing toward it.
The warm smell of kept blood and the tinny
smell of fresh blood would make any child quit
playing and wander in toward the skinny
feet, bulldog calves, and doe moose flanks planted
on either side of the porcelain bowl
below the blurry mons. The oxblood napkin landed
in the wastecan. The wise eyes of elephants roll
above their flanks, bellies, and rag-tear ears
in a permeable enormity of smell's
majesty and pungency; and benignity. Years
of months roll away what each month tells:
God, what animals we are, huge of haunch,
bloody and wise in the stench of bosk.

PETTING AND BEING A PET

Dogs, lambs, chickens, women—pets of all nations!
Fur or feathers under the kneading fingers
of those who long to have pets, relations
of softness to fleshiness, how a hand lingers
on a head or on the ear of a head, thus the sound
of petting and being a pet, a sounding horn:
needing met by kneading of bone which is found
through flesh. Have you ever felt forlorn
looking at a cat on someone else's lap, wishing
the cat was you? Look how an animal is passed
from lap to lap in a room, so many wishing
to hold it. We wish to be in the vast
caress, both animal and hand. Like eyes make sense
of seeing, touch makes being make sense.

WAKING TO THE CHATTER
OF THE CHILD NEXT DOOR

What interfered was the apartment wall
in the particular place the words tried
to get through. It was too thick. The shortened hall
is like four acoustic mirrors: to hide
sound is almost impossible, and yet
what the child wanted was so muffled
I couldn't discern what it was. Clouds, wet streets,
and a long, long bridge made of waffled steel
which seemed to elongate as I crossed it
toward a beautiful mountain, backlit,
were all elements of the dream in my mind
as I woke. The mountain was a purple
majesty mountain with the Japanese kind
of layered snow on top. As the child's warble
of "More!" woke me, I thought, more of what?
then saw the interminable bridge
and realized my neighbor's door had shut.
What I wanted to know in that sudden lurch
of consciousness was *everything more*
so I could answer what the child had asked for
because I'd rubbed its *more* through my dream's edge;
then I knew all this was my childhood search.

A BED FOR A WOMAN

I sat right up in bed and said, "Help."
I didn't scream it as if I were dreaming
a nightmare. I don't know what I was dreaming.
The "Help" came from a dream core like the pulp
in the core of a tooth. I wasn't frightened,
and that's important since it took all my
energy and self-concern to understand why
I spoke in the darkness but wasn't frightened.
I rose up out of bed like a person
whose fever had broken as this person
had known it would. Desperation,
hysterical shapelessness, was not in the word
as it would have been had I *called*, but I *spoke*.
"Help" was more like an answer. When I woke,
but not immediately, for I was too startled, I smiled
in this bed for a woman, far from the crib of a child.

AND YOU WERE A BABY GIRL

I loved your smell when you were a baby
high above me lying in your bassinet
amid cotton, flannel, and rubbery
talc. I stood in the mock diaper I'd wet
(a dishtowel pinned around my rear end) and sniffed
upward past the trousered and wool-skirted knees
toward you, taking in a uriney whiff
of the light but deep sweet smell of fleece
that was your infant skin thirty years ago.
When we lie close together now on the beach
on our towels in the wind near the undertow
in a flower of years whorled against the crease
of sand by the tin waves, I catch the tender
spark of the faint comet of your infant
smell, still, and am shocked and won't surrender
and then do—it is all the years have meant,
the damp baby smoke of rivalry unfurled
beyond the salt and oil of the practicing world.

ISLANDS IN OUR EYES

Islands are magical, like suns and moons,
surrounded by water, as suns and moons
are surrounded by nothingness, black cool space.
Eyes are islands surrounded by face.
Our isolation from the mainland makes
the thoughts inside us circles in lakes
mouthing plummeting stones. The middle
of the widening pupil of the riddle
is what the daily round taught you and me:
how to build a bridge right through the blank sea
and still come out standing, not just somewhere,
but on our island, finding what we want there.

SO, WHEN I SWIM TO THE SHORE

Living alone is like floating on blue
waters, arms out, legs down, in a wide bay
face to the sun on a brilliant white day,
the buildings of the city all around one,
millions of people doing what is done
in yellow buildings ringing a turquoise bay
in which one floats, in a lazy K
arms out, head back, legs spread beneath the brew
the clouds will make later on. One is
at the center of something of which one is
no more a part.

        So, when I swim to the shore
and go home and lie down, lips blue, cunt cold,
yet clitoris hard and blue and I am still
alone—never again your finger or lip
or knuckle or two fingers or tongue tip—
what do you think I will do? Send you a bill
for my service as a shill in the carney game
you played with your wife? Hell, let's tame
our own monsters. There's this in being out of love:
I own every blue day I'm not a part of.

CUT FLOWER

From the arms and stems of all the others,
the whole tribe of lilies swaying
as lilies of lilies together, all lovers,
an instinct inside it kept it swaying
away from what looked to me its rooted
place. Its silky orangeness in the vase, alone,
alone and in command of its unrooted
isolated state, was beautiful, for grown
full nakedness right where I could witness it
was beautiful, huge and proximate.
When I looked at it, I saw my better self
in the makeshift kingdom of a vase. In
cutting it, I cut myself from the swollen field,
out of what I was in, becoming alien.
Thus separation was the power I could wield.

AFRAID

Hell, I'm afraid I'll be afraid of your voice,
that's why I don't call (and because I'd like
to be grown-up about my phone bill, choice
being a signal of adulthood)! Like
something papery, but stiff, I think
your voice will sound, like the end of a tablet
of paper, no more whiteness or lines set
in sheer availability. My heart will sink
when I see the gray cardboard backing staring
at me, unblinking, the way I think your voice
will stare, if voices stared, gray and uncaring.
I wish you were here. I'd ask your advice
about whether to call. You'd put your arm
around me and we'd talk, our voices warm,
about whether it would do us any harm.

A FACE REGRESSES

I know that everyone becomes a child
sometimes, but the sunken image a face
becomes, like a small carved pumpkin with a wild
look to its eye in the moment before the trace
of light provided by the birthday candle
in its gut is snuffed out, the face of the child
lined and wizened that is the dry bundle
of wrinkles a grown face takes on, turning mild
everyday living into the knotted mass
of enemy, parent, baby, jealousy, needs,
is horrific in its turning—pass by friends, pass
by labors of years, pass hurt and love—and breeds
the sulphuric smell of snuffed candle and
vegetable rot that is aged desire,
the want to spark a need that, were it fanned
now, would never flame because the air
of the present will not satisfy it and
the air of the past never gratified its end.

CHILDREN AS ANCIENTS

The kids and I made an orchestra today.
I told them to form a circle, then asked
each one to make up a sound. My face masked
by god-likeness far above their fray,
I saw them all practicing their
shrill, recollected, sarcophagal sounds
like shards unearthed from ancient losts and founds
—the vibrating shards of their parents' nightmares
poking through the kids' bluish temples prayers
that flaked, then broke—harp-like and rare.
The room was a sound museum womb.
Never wanting to hear them again,
I crawled back into my own den
of ripened iniquity, a room
in my head beneath the stretched, papery
skin of my temples, my brain's nursery
where sounds were muffled by its drapery
of tissue and blood, where I was alone,
far away from the drone of the wizened,
miniaturized voices of my own
parents somehow coming through them, risen
into their mouths. I did not answer them
when they called me, all around me their rhythm.
I was sealed in the head of my own tomb.
They are not mine. They are not from my womb.
"OK, that's enough, kids," I said
and their sound went dead.

SKY INSIDE

To understand is to stand under the sky
of your own desires. Instincts are always
to grow. Watch that insane boy to see why
he shakes his hands and head and never plays.
He is too busy trying to grow through
the firestorm of terror that shakes him.
People who do not see you will watch you
and tell you what you are according to them,
self-destructive, or tortured, or any
one of the terms the mind employs to put
itself over the matter. The many
nodes of growth on your limbs are unseen; brute
pressure of the sap inside you makes you grow
while the worlds inside you smoke and blow.

SWEET TIME

The largest bud in creation travels
up the swollen stem of the amaryllis
like a ship in a womb up a river.
When it reaches its height, the bud unravels
so completely slowly that the thrill is
measured, pleasure by pleasure, each shiver
of the petals noted with the naked eye
noting that it is all naked and red
and about to, about to. Something will try
to surface: it is all about surfaces shed,
discovered, it is all about what wells up
in its own sweet time as sinless and sudden
and unfathomed as an old bad word in the cup
of the lips as a private part sits in a hand, unhidden.
Do you know what sin is? Sin is something
pried out before its time, unresolved unreadiness.
There are things that are properly buried
alive—not bones, not treasure—things living
that will emerge and won't be dug for. Their readiness
is making their own sweet ways unburied

THE VEIL OF IF

Isn't there a word for it? The fine wet
condensation on grapes and plums as if
each fruit were a soft upper lip furred with sweat:
that matte wrapping of moisture erased
with a finger or smeared by a thumb:
that coating, as if the color of the skin
had mixed with whitewash disguising each plum,
each holly of grapes, in the silk of a chaste
wet stocking? Transparency of desire.
Isn't there a word for it?

                            The handkerchief
or camisole of sweat on fruit on a spire
of a limb or a vine. The web ripeness spins.
A tangerine wrenched open, each section
fluttering on the rind like butterfly
wings on a bruised flower, or the erection
of the heads of raspberries: the almost shy
almost cry of Just Before: the drenched skein,
the cloud or web of moisture we rub
away on our way to the fruit. Dub
it protection, anticipation, pain
of If—before the certainties reign.

MENTAL FRANCE

We adults make love, but I am far away
in a hut at dusk where two lovers lay
swathed in orange light. Near night. A table
across the room, a purple swath of cloth
on the floor (a girl's dress), on the table
two green oranges . . . blur in my thought. Both
of us almost stop moving in the hiatus
that comes while we wait for each other to focus.

What I used to read is real.
The hut was in a book I read for hours
in school, praying to feel what other people feel.
Now that my desires suit my powers
I find a fresh past in this present, cut
from the literature of love like a fresh
wish clipped from a standard prayer: my hut
in France in this apartment of flesh.

NEXT AFTERNOON

The phlox is having fun, the purple phlox
is having fun, peonies are having fun,
the car is bouncing down the road, a box
of pansies overturns, the fox kit is having fun
catching bugs in the hay in the field
beyond the irises' purple yield
beyond the stream as the muffler warbles
when the car bounces down the bridge. And I
had fun, too. And so did you. Sex is a sort
of racing whitish purple at 3 A.M. Why
does love run so far to be near? No retort.
You're not here. The day's fun is a soft but clear
violet violence of were and we're.

CUTTING TALL GRASS

I love the sound of lawnmowers each year.
There's a woman in her workpants smelling of
gasoline and cut grass, wiping a smear
of grease on her head while blotting a swelling of
sweat from her head under her plastic visor.
I'm not sure whether she loves that machine.
Short grass is none the wiser for the razor,
so the love of mowing it is love of sheen.
But one must love the vehicle, the sun,
the bugs thrown up behind and the swallows
snatching bugs at the wheels to love a lawn,
the old grass spewn in the bleak shadows,
the new grass smelling of wet and slight rot,
to love to live between what is and is not.

A GARDEN

Whoever loves a garden fears seasons.
This is the highest of civilizations,
a bed in the earth. Great fears are the reasons
for each garden. Simple devastations—
fake death, false dreams, hungers only imagined
—are just the magic of habits compared
to fear of dirt nature, its crouch, the lesioned
back of earth. The swamp's spilled stomach is stared
down by eyes in a garden. Seasons terrify,
they terrify with their strict endurance
and strict abandonment, like parents. Why?
To garden is to love the instance, the dance
of one's reason and the season, a time
seized to be eased: a garden is a rhyme.

A GESTURE

Something kind done, something kind said
in spite of everything done and said, in spite
of a soreness of mind, is like being led
to a lawn edged with trees in partial light
where a cloth is spread out for a picnic
—or is it a towel? This is not a picture
but, surprised by sun, put together quick,
a meal of invention startled by nature
into being at all—a startled meal,
arrested on a beach towel, drumsticks,
a half-gone liter of wine—a gift of the real,
an imperfect, conscious attempt to fix
something wrong with something kind, beautiful
because the ragged haste of the gesture is full
of half-creation and suddenly wanting
to do something, since something was wanting.

THE BURNT LAWN

The August lawn is overmown; it's tan,
almost, instead of green. It's dry, not sad.
(It's not going to die.) Millions of bodies ran
through the lawn this summer: dogs, birds,
barefooted kids, and the feet of women
and men, strapped with tan marks from the sun.
The bare calves, fleecy heads, and lemon-
colored buttocks in the distance in the sun
of those two beautiful kids' bodies making
love rolled down the lawn while we watched with drinks
in our hands on the hill one day, taking
our time, taking all the world's time for the links
which would link you and me momentarily.
You noticed them first. I was talking too hurriedly.

NERVOUS JABBERING

When I lost my watch I thought I'd give up
time altogether. Going around with time
strapped to my wrist was too much to live up
to under the circumstances, and sublime
the circumstances were not: I bolted
my food, clawed into lines, slapped down money,
snapped open papers, walked on blisters, jolted
to halts before elevators, constant runny
nose and sore throat notwithstanding, a saint.
I was a saint when I lost my watch. Prime
life on the hoof. The watch itself was a cheap
little number that literally fell
off my wrist. How was I? Time couldn't tell.
Got to keep, got to keep, not saying what to keep
or who, how, or yet to keep is the talk of time.

AMONG TALL BUILDINGS

And nothing, not even that girl you love
with the mole on her arm, will be left. Huge
trenches will be dug just beyond the stove
the whole northeast corridor will become
and the dead will be piled in each rude gouge,
even that girl whose left ear always sticks
slightly out beyond her hair. To fix
the names of who died on tape won't be done
since they'll dig quick to prevent disease. Nobody
likes to hear this kind of talk. I always
hated to hear it myself until I began
loving the mortar between blocks, that cruddy
pocked cement holding up buildings so a man
and a woman can embrace in the maze
of what they've built on the errors of their ways.

AUBADE

The morning is lifted aloft by the praise
and prayers of birds without the noise
of even occasional traffic yet. "Mays"
lift the cloud of "may nots" that were night's voices—
mock, stock, quarrel, sorrow, and snarl. Fine
cries in the skies shout *Tomorrow!* So it is.
Darkness was not a cover. It was shame's time
beat to a rhyme of not/got. "Have" and "save" twist
in the clouds which bear aloft the morning
messages of words talked out loud in dreams
un- or dis- or half-remembered by darning
voices sewing holes that night poked in the seams
through which those words escaped and rose on wings so
to bear the day to what it seems, and sings so.

SUNNY DAYS

The children are singing a song about
morning where they all put their arms over
their heads to show the sun coming out,
then turn in their places, dip, then uncover
their arms to show the sun again. They are
all concentrating hard, the grown-up-acting
Spanish girls, the babyish blonder girls far-
ther into the room. All this is taxing
after numbering and reading and drawing
and praying and eating just right and sharing,
the polyester habit gently whirring
out from the hips of Sister Roseann. Carrying
the burden of always being sunny
is too hard. Yet the kids try for sunny:
begonias, Sister Roseann, recess, milk,
the weedy sidewalk, watching a pimp bilk
one of his girls on 6th Street and hearing
her shriek, watching one of the girls ignoring
Roseann, who grabs her, and hearing her shriek.
The meek scream and the masters are meek
as they bring mistakes to light. The girls take
darkness and put it behind their eyes. They make
homes for themselves behind their screams and lies.

THERE'S NO EARTHLY REASON

There's no earthly reason to be horrified
by the fact that we become like our parents.
Hell, we imitated all their nonsense
since we were born. We wanted to be, we tried
to be all grown, all free. We did what we saw.
We knew where the hand went on that hip,
how the Lucky dangled from that lower lip.
What we saw in their eyes was our law.
Their pain was our pain, ours unmitigated
by their circumstance. We were the little whales
who swallowed them whole, our Jonahs who waited
to be digested by our tiny tracts. What fails
to get digested, the Jonah eye, or Jonah limb
or knuckle, the part we took in but couldn't
break down, the tooth of their essence in our dim
interior, is what we puke up or pass out
and what makes us free, the "them" we couldn't
make into the "me." Yet, we tie about
our bodies their lovely or ugly trappings.
These are our parents' unwrappings,
still warm and still smelling of another's body,
and it seems, sometimes, that we are what we loathed
because of how we've chosen to be clothed.
It's that we put on what we wouldn't take in,
because it wasn't ours. It was just imitation
of emotion, the body we used to study.

BERRIES WHICH ARE BERRIES

A pink plastic bowlful of blackberries—
transported among the enlarged knuckles
of a hand moving past the Marys
and Jesuses on the calendars buckled
to the flowery walls, then dropped on the oilcloth
in front of me, berry juice dripping off
the arthritic knuckles onto the oilcloth,
and berry juice staining the inside walls of
the bowl a blue like ships-far-out-in-the-sea
—was my breakfast. *"Breakfast!"* "Hi, Gram."
Freedom felt as if it swelled beneath me,
sea-like swells of is, are, and am.
I am free today thinking of that moment,
because the thought of our summer routine
frees me as a metronome saves time
by measuring: each thing meaning what it meant.

THE LITTLE GIRLS

Listening to the voice of an older child
informing a younger child of a "fact"
the kid didn't know, and watching the wild
parental look of the older one and the act
of guarded nonchalance the younger one puts on
changes their colored world into black and white.
The ordinary chrome of days gets wan,
then gray, then just as black as houses at night,
door after door shut, black as forgetting.
The older one's helpless face contorts in
its official meanness, hungry and aggrieved.
The younger face, after the brief bloodletting
(a high-pitched minute of mocking) reports in
for adult ammunition. Both are bereaved.

THE WEB OF HISTORIES

The sadness that prevails among families
is the web of histories spun, fibrous
and intense and wet, then dried. It multiplies
its strands to the gossamer stickiness
of the web on the handle of an unused
pump in an unlit pumproom used only
in July, when the running waterworks, fused
from temporary drought, don't work. Lonely
spider, catching bugs calmly in the dust,
leaves quick as water dives into the bucket,
leaving you to tear and catch at the web—lust
is a sticky mess—all over your arms. "Fuck it!"
and the door slams shut, leaving you dripping
a bucket into the light, swearing and half weeping.

MY VAST PRESUMPTION

The balloon ride was his birthday present
three years ago. He never cashed the ticket,
I know, because periodically I'm sent
reminders in the mail. "I didn't take it,
not yet," he said for nearly a year. We don't
bring it up any more. I thought I'd try
a rescue, thought I should—the mire he was in,
his father, his job. Since we were kids, a lie
was a sin, still is. He's my favorite cousin.
I'd love to see him way up in the air
billowed over the farms below, the red stripes
teetering from cloud to cloud, from when to where,
far away from bleak here. "I'm not the type,"
he finally said from his own balloon,
never waving, since never leaving home,
the faintly hysterical first goodbye,
"See you again, soon!"

STUMBLE

Because you've tumbled off what you were on,
for a minute you forget where you're from.
Stumble and bumble. Where will you be
in 2003? What will you see?
Will you have any money? Will you be
where you thought you ought to have been before?
That shit's always at the door. Fate's in the dirt
you dust off your skirt after you fall. It's in
the picayune baby tears your mother, alert
to every change in the weather, rubbed in
your skin, thinking to wipe the tears off. Fate
is overturning: seeing sky instead
of straight ahead. A stumble weans us from the state
of overweening plans, of the leadened, dead
exactitude of schedule. Remember all
the centuries you fall on when you fall.

NOVEMBERS

Novembers were the months that began with No.
"Oh no." They died in embers. Above were
V's of geese in skies lit from these low
Even fires. The fires of fall were
Mirrors for the feelings I felt before
Being. I'm telling you now I feel I
Exist for the first time! Neither the bareness nor
Roughness demoralize—I realize I
See much clearer what leafless branches show.

THIS TIME

All the light, all the bare trees, all the clean
windows through which the light through the trees comes,
this is my home. There comes my sister, unseen
through the empty woods, then visible; there comes
my mother slowly through the sunlight; through
the open door my cousin comes, unlacing
his boots. It is as if we are all new
with the newness spring has, a season's spacing
of newness among oldnesses remade,
each "again" made fresh from old "agains." The light
is so full of air, it seems we are made
of air, as the space that is home in our sight
is made of time. Home is the space
so filled with time that time stands still
for it is contained there. Home is where the will
becomes visible. Just as we can see air's face
when it is wind knocking against branches,
time becomes material, and my cousin blanches
at my sister's remark remade from an old
slight, except it is this time, old time controlled.

DESIRE

It doesn't speak and it isn't schooled,
like a small foetal animal with wettened fur.
It is the blind instinct for life unruled,
visceral frankincense and animal myrrh.
It is what babies bring to kings,
an eyes-shut, ears-shut medicine of the heart
that smells and touches endings and beginnings
without the details of time's experienced *part-
fit-into-part-fit-into-part.* Like a paw,
it is blunt; like a pet who knows you
and nudges your knee with its snout—but more raw
and blinder and younger and more divine, too,
than the tamed wild—it's the drive for what is real,
deeper than the brain's detail: the drive to feel.

WORLD WE SLEEP IN

There's no one to watch us and grin at us
as we scratch each other's asses and smalls
of backs in the blind way of sleep, phallus
breathing in the Y of the thighs, and walls
about us breathing, no one to look down,
like God, enjoying the view in His way,
curling His nostril and lip to frown
at the profane beauty of how we lay
in our bed of beds. The two college kids
who are not our children and who have not
come home for school vacation making bids
for our attention by flinging open—"What?"
"Look at them."—the bedroom door, then stopping,
pleased only as our pleasure reflects on them,
are not watching us. Without God or popping
eyes of sophomores, no one lifts the hem
of our privacy. It is a godless,
childless world we sleep in, relieved that we
are relieved of faith and responsibility,
though that means there's no one to watch us
and therefore bless us. And so I clamber
through my eyes, then fly out from my head
to bless, if I can, our sheeted chamber,
gawking from the ceiling at us in our bed.

FORSYTHIA BELOW CLOUDS

What chases spring? Almost anything.
Wind chases it into place, of course, every
chance it gets. Pennies in a pocket, jingling
forgotten in a cotton jacket chase it. Shivery
afternoons chasing dusk chase spring. The yawns
of a million people each act as a million
miniature bellows blowing ninety downs
into bloom, and each dawn catches the loose pollen
of spring in its pastel cup. Winter chases
spring into place like an aging annoyed
Angora cuffs its offspring. It erases
anything cosy. Spring is a colder void,
actually, because of its light. Getting
ready, chasing things away by chasing
them into place, involves cold, light erasing.
Spring is a way of embracing forgetting.

THE BREACH OF *OR*

Broken lines continue, you know, way past
their breaks, as medians in roads do, or
the dot tracings in kids' books, where the last
point is the first point. But it's the breach of *or*,
the breach a break makes when it skids into
nothingness that I'm panicked will undo
me into an ennervated void.
That's why I love you; it's how I avoid
the blank *or* between the black lines. That's why
I love my friends. Taking a pencil with
a heavy lead that will leave a line, wide
and black in its wake, connects given lines with
something almost equal to them. Imagine
a little boat trying to connect two
shores with its wake. It's futile. Now look in
the boat at the picnickers, those two
lovers crowded among pears, cantaloupes, fried
squid and fluttering, flag-like, paper napkins—
watch them wipe their lips, open their arms wide,
embracing each other, laughing about their sins.
A pencil made this. Black lines tried
to equal them. The void was a matter of my pride.

MOLLY PEACOCK was born in Buffalo, New York, in 1947. She graduated from the State University of New York at Binghamton and was a Danforth Fellow at Johns Hopkins. Her first collection of poems, *And Live Apart*, was published by the University of Missouri Press in 1980. The poems in *Raw Heaven* have appeared in *The New Yorker*, the *Paris Review*, *Shenandoah* and other leading literary magazines. Ms. Peacock currently lives in New York City, where she teaches at Friends Seminary.